I know this to be true

NELSON MANDELA
FOUNDATION
Living the legacy

Bryan Stevenson

I know this to be true

---

on equality,
justice &
compassion

Interview and photography
Geoff Blackwell

CHRONICLE BOOKS
SAN FRANCISCO

in association with

Blackwell&Ruth.

Dedicated to the legacy
and memory of
Nelson Mandela

'Ultimately you judge the character of a society not by how they treat the rich and the powerful and the privileged, but by how they treat the poor. The condemned. The incarcerated. Because it's in that nexus that we truly begin to understand truly profound things about who we are.'

Introduction

In July 1989 Bryan Stevenson received a phone call from Holman Correctional Facility in Alabama, USA. The man at the end of the line was Herbert Richardson, an African American death row inmate whose execution was scheduled for one month's time. He begged Stevenson to represent him. If there was no hope, he said, he didn't know how he could go on. Over the weeks that followed Stevenson made numerous attempts to stay the execution. The response was always the same: it's too late.

Richardson was a Vietnam War veteran who suffered from post-traumatic stress disorder. His mother had died when he was a small child and he had a history of drug and alcohol abuse. In a misguided bid to win his ex-girlfriend back, he had placed a homemade bomb on her porch in the hope that he would save her, and that they would rekindle their relationship. Instead, her young niece picked up the bomb and was killed instantly by the explosion. Despite his history of trauma and an obvious lack of intention to kill, Richardson was sentenced to death.

Stevenson stayed with him in the minutes before his execution. He was distressed, upset, and humiliated from having the hair shaved off his body. They prayed together and hugged, and, on 19 August 1989 at 12:14 a.m., Richardson died by electric chair. He was forty-three.

This case is just one of many that Bryan Stevenson has encountered throughout his long career as a public interest lawyer. But it had a profound impact – it transformed the way he thought about the death penalty and it fuelled him in his fight to avoid execution for death row prisoners.

'The death penalty isn't about whether people deserve to die . . . I think the threshold question is: Do we deserve to kill?'

Stevenson grew up in the shadow of racial injustice. His great-grandparents had been born into slavery and he was raised in a racially segregated community in rural Delaware. As a law school graduate working for the Southern Prisoners Defense Committee in Atlanta, Georgia, USA, he encountered racial prejudice and oppression time and again – not just in the cases he took, but at times in his personal treatment from white members of authority.

After co-founding the Equal Justice Initiative (EJI) in 1989, the injustices he was confronted with grew at a rapid pace. Located in Montgomery, Alabama, USA, EJI is a non-profit law centre that provides free legal aid to death row prisoners. As the organization expanded, its programme broadened to include excessive punishment, wrongful convictions, children sentenced to life in prison without possibility of parole, and mentally ill prisoners who were sentenced without their mental state being taken into consideration.

Stevenson has been guided by an unwavering belief that the worst things that happen to a person shouldn't define their life. Every person has the capacity to change and deserves the opportunity for redemption. Every person deserves to be treated equally. Yet for African Americans, this is not the case. 'Our society applies a presumption of dangerousness and guilt to young black men, and that's what leads to wrongful arrests and wrongful convictions and wrongful death sentences, not just wrongful shootings. There's no question that we have a long history of seeing people through this lens of racial difference. It's a direct line from slavery to the treatment of black suspects today, and we need to acknowledge the shamefulness of that history.'[1]

Walter McMillian is an example of this historic discrimination. McMillian had been sentenced to death for the 1986 murder of Ronda Morrison, an eighteen-year-old white woman from Monroeville, Alabama. Despite having a solid alibi and multiple witnesses to confirm it, McMillian was targeted by local authorities who were under pressure to make an arrest. He had gained a reputation in the community for having an interracial affair with a married woman, earning the resentment of certain white locals.

With only the false testimonies of two career criminals and no physical evidence against him, McMillian was convicted of capital murder by a white-majority jury. The white judge, Robert E. Lee Key, used judicial override – a practice legal in Alabama until 2017 – to rescind the jury's recommendation of a life sentence and impose capital punishment.[i] When twenty-eight-year-old Stevenson first took the case, he received a phone call from Key, who tried to persuade him not to represent McMillian. Ignoring the judge's advice, he persevered.

Faced with corruption and challenges at every turn – and even multiple bomb threats – Stevenson and his colleague, Michael O'Connor, remained determined in their quest to free an innocent man condemned to die. After years of work, they succeeded, and McMillian was exonerated in 1993. His freedom was a compelling example of justice, and his resilience a vital reminder of the power of hope and forgiveness. 'Walter had taught me that mercy is just when it is rooted in hopefulness and freely given. Mercy is most empowering, liberating, and transformative when it is directed at the undeserving,' Stevenson writes in his book, *Just Mercy: A Story of Justice and Redemption*. 'Walter genuinely forgave the people who unfairly accused him, the people who convicted him, and the people who judged him unworthy of mercy. And in the end, it was just mercy toward others that allowed him to recover a life worth celebrating.'[2]

Stevenson has made a career out of standing up for people like McMillian – the oppressed, the marginalized and the voiceless. For over thirty years he has tirelessly fought for social justice and emphasized the ingrained nature of institutional racism in America. During this time he has won relief, reversals or release for more than 135 prisoners, and has helped achieve a US Supreme Court ruling that banned life in prison without parole sentences for children. But it isn't just his track record that should be acknowledged, nor his remarkable ability to highlight the urgent need to reform the American criminal justice system.

More than that, it's his capacity to imagine a light at the end of the tunnel even when it may seem that things will be dark forever. It's his belief that there is potential for good present in every person and his belief in the necessity of second chances. It's his faith in the fundamental power of truth. Stevenson proves that change can be made, that justice can be found, and that there is always hope. That even in the face of great odds, good can prevail.

'I have discovered, deep in the hearts of many condemned and incarcerated people, the scattered traces of hope and humanity – the seeds of restoration that come to astonishing life when nurtured by very simple interventions.'[3]

'We talk a lot about freedom.
We talk a lot about equality.
We talk a lot about justice.
But we're not free. There are
shadows that follow us.'

The Interview

What really matters to you?

I think fairness matters, equality matters,
justice matters. I can't change the history of
the world – which has been for many people
so unfair, so unjust – but I can, hopefully,
contribute to systems and structures and
ways of thinking, and acting, that eliminate
unfairness, and eliminate injustice and
inequality. I think that matters.

Obviously there are basic human
relationships that matter to all of us, but when
those relationships are constrained by the
structural inequality of systemic oppression,
I just think we don't get to live the full human
existence that we're meant to live. I want to
do what I can to make that *full* human life
available to as many people as possible.

I actually love seeing the justice quotient
increase in a community; I love seeing people
recover from years or decades of unfairness,
with something that feels like real change.
That energizes me, that animates my work
and my life.

Did you have a particular ambition or aspiration
as a young person?

As a small kid, I don't think I was unlike most
kids. I wanted to be a baseball player, and
if not a baseball player, a basketball player.
I got involved in music very early, and so if
I wasn't going to be an athlete I wanted to be
a musician. I think you get to a point where
you begin to doubt whether that's really going
to happen. I didn't really have aspirations
beyond that; I wasn't somebody who grew
up thinking, 'I want to be a lawyer.' In fact
I never met a lawyer until I got to law school.
Law school was sort of a default. I was a
philosophy major in college, and got to the
end of my college years and realized that
nobody was going to pay me to philosophize.

I looked into graduate school and was
shocked to learn that to go to graduate school
in this country and pursue a degree in history
or English or political science, you actually
have to know something about history,
English or political science. I ended up in law
school because you don't really need to know
anything to go to law school. I was quite

disillusioned there until I met people on death row, until I got exposed to the sort of work that I do now. But I didn't have a really clear plan. I knew wanted to help people, I wanted to respond to the inequality and injustice that I grew up with. But I didn't have a very specific idea about *how*.

I was very moved by people who found a way to help other people, and not just famous people, but people in my community. Those old mothers who would feed you, even if they had just a little bit left in the cupboard, they would make space for you. People who would embrace you even if they didn't know you, if they saw you were in pain or you were in need. That's the thing I witnessed that really shaped me.

I guess my aspiration was just to become one of those people who would pick up someone who falls down, who would embrace someone who was struggling, who would encourage someone who's lost their way, who would represent the possibility of triumph and justice even in the face of a lot of inequality and injustice.

Has there been a special individual or individuals that have particularly inspired you by their example or wisdom?

My grandmother. I talk about my grandmother a lot because she was absolutely a force in our family. She was really strategic, and smart. She was tough, she was strong, but she was kind, and she was loving. I tell stories about her all the time, because they were so formative for me.

When integration came to our community, it created a lot of anxiety. We weren't sure what was going to happen when black kids were finally going to have the chance to go to the public schools. I started my education at a coloured school. I think she was worried; she never grew up in an integrated environment. And so, after integration was announced, my grandmother started doing this thing where she would come up to me before we would go to school, and she would give me these hugs. She'd squeeze me so tightly I thought she was trying to hurt me. Then she'd see me an hour later and say, 'Bryan, do you still feel me hugging you?' And if I said, 'No,' she would jump on me again. After a couple of months, I had learned that every time I see my grandmother, the first thing I would say is, 'Mama, I always feel you hugging me.' And she'd smile this smile, and I didn't appreciate what she was doing until much, much later.

She was a domestic, she cleaned other people's homes. She lived into her nineties – but when she was in her nineties she fell, she broke her hip, and she was diagnosed with cancer. She was dying when I was in college and I went to see her, and it was really hard because she meant the world to me. I was sitting there, and I was just saying all of these things, and holding her hand. Her eyes were closed – I wasn't even sure she could hear what I was saying. But it came time to leave, and I knew I had to go. I got up to leave, and just before I walked away, my grandmother opened her eyes, and she squeezed my hand and looked at me, and the last thing she said was, 'Bryan, do you still feel me hugging you?' And then she said, 'I want you to know I'm always going to be hugging you.' There have been many times in my life when I have felt the embrace of that woman.

It's this power that comes from this love forged by struggle and adversity, but relentlessly committed to caring and nurturing, and the well-being of those you bring into the world, that has really inspired me more than anything. I think about the fact that her parents were enslaved, and she was terrorized and fled Virginia for the north, and never got to vote, never got to do these things that she desperately wanted to do. She had to endure all of that humiliation and indignation of Jim Crow laws, seeing those signs.[ii] And yet she had this charity, and generosity of spirit. That inspired me; people like my grandmother inspire me. Even people whose names I didn't know, but represented the orientation of my grandmother, inspired me.

I used to be a church musician as a young kid. I'd play in these testimonial services – people would come in, and they would often have heartbreaking testimonies. They would talk about how they didn't have enough food for their family that week, and somebody was missing, and all kinds of challenges, or there had been violence in the home; they'd give these heartbreaking testimonies. But then they would stand up and start singing,

'But I wouldn't take nothing from my journey now.'[iii] That spirit, that will, that commitment to struggle, and to overcome, very much inspired me. So, I think about these women, and some men, who were around me as a child, as my true heroes, my true source of inspiration.

*

I'm definitely a product of the people who have come before me. My great-grandfather was enslaved, but he was very verbal – he learned to read as a twelve-year-old, even though it could have cost him his life as an enslaved person to know how to read. But because of that, after emancipation, enslaved people would come to his home and he would read the newspaper every night. My grandmother would tell me these stories of how proud she was that he would read the newspaper, and it made her want to read, and she taught my mother how to read. My mom had this thing about reading, and we were so poor, but she went into debt to buy the *World Book Encyclopedias* so that we could read and have access to the world.

'We change the world when the ideas in our minds are fuelled by the conviction in our hearts.'

When you see people you love and care about organizing themselves around these ideas, it has a huge impact. The people in my community were disfavoured, they were excluded, we were racially segregated. We were effectively told that our lives weren't as valuable or as meaningful as other people's lives; that we're not as hard working, or as smart. When you see how people really *are* hard-working, and they really are committed, they are smart, and they're not allowed to express that – that creates a consciousness that will push you, that will drive you. I think that certainly motivated me.

When integration came I really wanted to prove to people that our community represented something healthy, and beautiful, and necessary. When I met other people who came out of circumstances like mine, I wanted to respond to that. I do think that I've always stood on the shoulders of people who did so much more with so much less. That has made it really hard for me to not contribute, to not do what I can in the life that I've been given. I look back a lot, and I think about all of the anguish and suffering, and inequality

that people experienced, and yet found a way
to keep pushing, to love, to be hopeful. That
animates my work in life, and motivates me
to do the same for the generations to come.

What are the daily disciplines and routines
you practice?

Well I do think you can be motivated by a lot
of things. You can, if you're not careful, be
consumed with anger and animosity towards
those who have perpetrated all of these issues.
But for me, there's a Niebuhr quote, "Love
is the motive, but justice is the instrument."[iv]
I think, ultimately, I have been taught that you
have to stay on the side of love. It's not easy,
but if you allow yourself to be consumed with
hatred and anger, it will actually disrupt your
ability to love even the people who are not
your enemies, who are not perpetrating these
atrocities. You end up in this place where love
is diminished, and when that happens, you
don't get to be a full human being.

That's what's so fascinating about the
history, particularly of African Americans
in this country. When emancipation came,

African Americans had every right to hate those who had oppressed and enslaved them. They could have said, 'We want revenge.' But what they said instead was, 'We just want an opportunity.' They had this instinct for reconciliation, even when it wasn't rational. Despite that, they were terrorized and tormented, traumatized by decades of lynching and violence. And even during that time period, people didn't say, 'It's time to just die and revolt.' They kept trying to persuade, they actually kept appealing towards something that would allow for community. They didn't want vengeance, they just wanted security.

I think about Dr. King, and the people in this community who led the extraordinary civil rights movement[v] – it would have been much simpler to say, 'Let's burn the busses down, let's disrupt all of these institutions that disfavour us.' But they actually had enough love in their hearts that they were trying to encourage the rest of the community to see that it's not in their interest either to be so motivated and shaped by bigotry. I think that historical narrative has caused me to recognize it's not just something people do because it's convenient, it's not because they're not courageous, it's not because it's functional, it's not because it's easy. It has been because there is, at the heart of it, a basic recognition that to stay on the side of love, you cannot be shaped and driven by hatred. It can't be an 'eye for an eye', we'll just all be blind. It can't be this, 'You hit me, I hit you back. You kill me, I kill you back' mindset. And the great transformative models of true justice that we see around the world are models that are rooted in something that gets beyond hate and bigotry and oppression and mistreatment; [something] that is reparatory, that values redemption, and reconciliation, and restoration.

I have fallen down enough to know that when I fall down, I want a second chance, I want to be redeemed. I can't want that for myself and not give it to others. We don't have to be unkind as we work through issues and problems. We don't have to hate, we don't have to be consumed by violence. I just think it's a destructive path that doesn't allow you to succeed, or to be a full human in the way that we're intended to be.

Do you have guiding principles or a driving
philosophy that underpins your life and
decisions?

I am committed to this idea that to change the
world, to create justice, we have to be willing
to get proximate to the people we serve, to
the communities that are in need. I believe
very much in this notion of proximity – that we
can't actually be advocates, and provide aid,
if we are distant from the people we're trying
to serve. I actually think we learn things about
the problem only when we're proximate to
those who are suffering from those problems.
Our politicians fail us because oftentimes
their solutions are created from a distance.
When you are proximate, you hear things that
you can't hear from far away. You see things
that you can't see from far away. I actually
think that in proximity we learn what we
need to know about how to help. I don't think
you have to have answers, you can't come
in with solutions, you actually get solutions
in proximity.

I also believe that there are narratives
underneath the policy issues that tend to rage

in countries, and around the world, and we too often are so focused on the debates and the issues, that we're not listening for the narratives underneath the debates and the issues. I think that we have to pay attention to the underlying narratives, and we have to work on changing those narratives.

For example, in this country we have mass incarceration because we declared this misguided war on drugs. We said that people who are drug-addicted and drug-dependent are criminals, and because they're criminals, we're going to use the criminal justice system to punish those people. Now we didn't have to make that choice; we could have said that people with drug addiction and drug dependence have a health problem, that we need our healthcare system to respond to that problem. And the reason why I think we called them criminals instead of calling them sick has to do with politics of fear and anger. There is a narrative underneath that policy debate that was rooted in those politics.

I think fear and anger are the essential ingredients of oppression, and injustice, and inequality. When we allow ourselves to be

'It breaks my heart having to still say to black or brown kids that it doesn't matter if you're kind or hardworking, you're still going to go places where you're going to have to navigate the danger of being killed; you're going to have to be in total control when a police officer suspects you.'

governed by fear and anger, we tolerate things
we shouldn't tolerate. We accept things we
shouldn't accept. If you go anywhere in the
world where there's oppression and abuse,
and you ask the oppressor why they do what
they do, they'll give you a narrative of fear and
anger. Sustaining apartheid was defended by
the politics of fear and anger. The Holocaust
was justified by fear and anger. The genocide
in Rwanda. All of these problems have at
the heart this narrative of fear and anger.
So, I think we have to change that narrative.
I'm trying to change the narrative of racial
inequality in this country.

We're not free in America, we're
burdened by a history of racial inequality
that's created a kind of smog in the air. We've
practiced silence for so long that we're going
to have to disrupt that silence by talking about
things we haven't talked about before. I think
we're a post-genocide society in the United
States. I think when Europeans came to this
continent, we slaughtered millions of native
people; it was a genocide. But we created
this narrative of racial difference. We said that
native people were savages and justified that

violence. It was that narrative that created
centuries of enslavement. I don't think the
true evil of American slavery was involuntary
servitude and forced labour. I think it was this
ideology of white supremacy, this idea that
black people aren't the same as white people;
that we're not as good as white people.
And so confronting narratives, changing
narratives, is really important for me. That's
why we've built a museum, that's why we've
built a memorial.[vi] There's a presumption of
dangerousness and guilt that gets assigned to
black people in this country. Until we confront
that, and challenge it, and the narratives that
have sustained it, we're not going to get to
where we want to go.

I think my third principle is that we have
to be helpful. I don't think you can change
the world, or do justice, if you allow yourself
to become hopeless. I actually think that
hopelessness is the enemy of justice. Justice
prevails where hopelessness persists. And so,
your hope is your superpower, your hope is
what allows you to stand up when others say
sit down. It's what allows you to speak when
other people say, 'Be quiet.' It's an orientation

of the spirit. It's not a 'pie in the sky' thing.
This is how you stand in the face of adversity
and difficulty.

For me, it's been necessary to believe
things I've haven't seen my entire life.
I never met a lawyer until I got to law school.
I created this law project in a state that was
very hostile to the rights of people on death
row. Even building cultural sites [as] a law
non-profit seemed pretty improbable to a lot
of people. But we have this hope, and I think
that's key.

And then finally, I believe you've got to
be willing to do things that are uncomfortable
and inconvenient. Change does not happen,
justice does not happen, if you only do the
things that are comfortable and convenient.
Because we're human, and biologically and
psychologically programmed to do what's
comfortable, that means that we actually
have to make a choice to do uncomfortable
things. That requires some focus, and some
deliberation, and a little bit of courage. But
I am persuaded that that is key to how we
create healthier communities. I don't like it,
but I accept it as necessary. I've done some

research, I've looked for some examples where justice prevailed and equality triumphed and liberty won, and nobody had to do anything uncomfortable and inconvenient – and I can't find any examples of that. For me, this becomes a necessary part of it.

The beautiful thing is that we are surrounded by so many people who have been proximate, who have changed narratives, who have stayed hopeful, who have done uncomfortable things. I have worked in Montgomery, Alabama. It's a challenging place, but it's also an inspiring place. I could look out of my window when I'm feeling a little pushed and think about the people who were doing this work sixty years ago. They frequently had to say, 'My head is bloody but not bowed.'[vii] I've never had to say that. It just reminds me that I don't have a reason sufficient to stop given the things that people have done before me. Being proximate, changing narratives, staying hopeful, and doing uncomfortable things are really essential to how I believe justice can succeed, and equality can be achieved.

What qualities have been most critical to achieving goals during your life and career?

I think you have to be willing to accept help, and embrace help where you can get it. I started with virtually no staff, and had a really hard time getting people to join. Over time, that's changed. I'm really fortunate that we have a whole community of mission-driven people. It wasn't something we could demand. It wasn't even something we could expect, but it happened because we were open to it.

I think you have to be strategic; when you're dealing with big problems, you can't just do the thing you immediately want to do when you see inequality and injustice. You can't just be reactive. You have to think about, 'What's the proactive thing we can do that will really have an impact?' I think you have to put the people you serve first, and always be thinking about what their needs are, which are not always aligned to what your needs are. When you are client-centred, when you are service-centred, you make different choices than you might otherwise make.

And then I think you have to love what you do. I hate that I'm in a state that has such a horrible history of inequality, such a brutal history of lethal violence and punishment directed at disfavoured communities. I hate that I'm in a state with a level of poverty that is so great, where there's so much inequality and suffering. But I love that I have just a little bit that I can give in response to these problems, and that I'm allowed to do it, that I've been able to do it. For me, that gives me joy. It makes me feel like my life has meaning and purpose, and value. And humans that can live lives they believe are purposeful, that are valuable, that are joyful, are really the privileged people among us.

Being able to see the value in what we try to do has made it incredibly meaningful and affirming. When you feel affirmed in that way, it really does allow you to kind of take on things that you might not otherwise be willing to take on. Service is at the heart of it; I really think prioritizing the needs of the people you serve can orient you in ways that are critical for doing what we've been trying to do.

What are the biggest lessons you have learned during the course of your life and career?

I think you've got to be courageous. Sometimes you have to stand when other people say 'Sit down.' Sometimes you have to speak when other people say 'Be quiet.' That means you're going to have to be brave. You can't be shaped entirely by the ideas in your mind – we all need as much information as we can possibly get. We want to be informed, we want to be strategic, we want to be tactical. It's important that we understand the complexities.

But ultimately, I don't think we change the world with the ideas in our minds; we change the world when the ideas in our minds are fuelled by the conviction in our hearts. For me that means listening to your heart; what's right, what's fair, what's just. Even if there are strategies that might be effective, that are inconsistent with fair and just and right conduct, I think we have to step back from those. I think being motivated and led by the heart as well as the mind [is important].

The last one is that sometimes, you
have to position yourself in uncomfortable
places, difficult places, and you just have to
be a witness. Havel talked about this.[viii]
He said that during the time of Soviet
domination of Eastern Europe they wanted
recognition, they wanted money, they wanted
people to acknowledge the struggle they
were engaged in. He said that the only thing
they needed was hope. He says hope isn't
a preference of optimism over pessimism,
it's an 'orientation of the spirit'. It's the
willingness to position yourself in sometimes
hopeless places and be a witness. There is
something powerful about witness, about
representing human rights, about representing
human dignity, equality, justice, fairness, and
even redemption. That call to be a witness
has become even more critical to my own
thinking, and my own work.

'I think if most people saw what I see on a daily basis when I go into jails or prisons, if they were in the room and trying to respond to children who have been put in adult facilities, I don't think they would think differently than I do.'

Can you describe a key moment or crisis which
has particularly tested you?

I have lots of crises. There have been times –
I write about this – when we've had people
facing execution.[ix] When I first opened this
project [the Equal Justice Initiative] in 1989,
there was a man scheduled to be executed
in thirty days. We didn't have books, we
didn't have staff, we weren't really in a place
to take cases yet. He called me and said,
'Mr. Stevenson, will you please take my
case?' I said, 'I'm sorry but we don't have
books or staff, I can't do anything yet.' And he
was very quiet, and he hung up the phone.
I was really unnerved by the conversation,
I didn't sleep much that night.

I came back the next day and the man
called me again, and he said, 'Mr. Stevenson,
I know what you told me about not having
your books, and your staff, and your lawyers,
but I'm begging you – please take my case.
You don't have to tell me you can win, you don't
have to tell me you can stop the execution.
But I don't think I can make it in the next
twenty-nine days if there's no hope at all.'

And so, when he put it like that, I couldn't say no. So I said yes, and we tried really hard to stop the execution. But it was very late in the process, every court said, 'Too late. Too late. Too late.'

And on the day of the execution, I got the call from the Supreme Court telling me that our motion for stay had been denied. This man had asked me to be with him. So I drove down to Holman Prison – this is when they were executing people by the electric chair, a brutal, violent way to kill someone. When I got there, they shaved the hair off his body, and he was just so humiliated by that. And we were struggling, he was emotional, I was emotional. We were talking, and praying, and crying. And then he said to me, 'Bryan, it's been such a strange day.' He said, 'All day long people have been saying, "What can I do to help you?" This morning they came to me and said, "What can I get you for breakfast?" At midday, they came to me and said, "What do you want for lunch?" In the evening they came to me and said, "What can we get you for dinner?"' He said, 'Bryan, all day long, "Can we get you coffee? Can we get you water? Can we get you stamps to mail your letters? Can we get you the phone?"'

And I was standing there holding that man's hands, when he said, 'Bryan, it's been so strange. More people have asked me, "What can I do to help you?" in the last fourteen hours of my life than they ever did in the first nineteen years of my life.' Holding that man's hands I couldn't help but think, 'Where were they when you were three, being physically abused? Where were they when you were six, being sexually assaulted? Where were they at nine, when your mom died? Where were they when you were a teenager, drug-addicted? Where were they when you came back from Vietnam, traumatized and disoriented?' I know where they were when you were accused of a crime. They were lined up to execute you. And with those kinds of questions resonating in my mind, it was really, really difficult to have this man pulled away, strapped into an electric chair, and executed. I was haunted by that.

He was a Vietnam vet, and there was something about the way he thanked me for being in that space with him that made me begin to see the struggle in a very different way. I realized that the death penalty isn't about whether people deserve to die. I don't think that's the relevant threshold question. I think the threshold question is, 'Do we deserve to kill?' When you have a system of justice that treats people better if you're rich and guilty than if you're poor and innocent; when you have a system of justice that is shaped by economics; when you have a system that's shaped by politics, that's defined by error, you realize that the problem isn't entirely what *he* did, it's what *we're* doing.

Even in that moment of crisis, I felt like what I have to do is align myself with the condemned and the incarcerated and the excluded, even though it's a painful place to stand. It's a difficult place to stand. But if I believe, as I do, that we are all more than the worst thing we've ever done – that if someone tells a lie, they're not just a liar; or if they take something, that they're not just a thief; even if you kill someone, you're not just a killer – then I have to stand with those who have been accused, and suspected, and convicted, and condemned, and advocate for the other things they are.

It was challenging and hard, but necessary to find my way to the place we are now. We've had a lot of success, we've won a lot of cases – we don't win them all – but I think sometimes it's when you realize that you can't measure a journey by a straight line, you've got to measure the valleys, you've got to measure the hills. You've got to measure all of the crooked and difficult places to really evaluate what the path is, what the journey is. That's certainly been true for me. And I can't pull out those moments when I've been overwhelmed, and beat down, and heavily burdened by what my client has gone through, from getting to this place where we're trying to do what we're trying to do.

How do you deal with mistakes you've made or endeavours that have failed?

I think you have to be prepared for a certain quantum of missteps. Otherwise you become so risk-averse that you don't do anything. If you don't take risk, if you don't try to achieve things that haven't been achieved before, you don't actually help people in the way that they need help. When you orient yourself that way you will make mistakes, not everything will work.

It's funny, I feel like human history is a great teacher. So many of the people who have inspired me are the people who had the courage to sometimes err; to sometimes engage in a strategy that didn't work. All of that is part of what informs what I'm trying to do. Dr. King went to Albany, Georgia, and was not successful in achieving desegregation. But what he learned in Albany is what shaped what came in Selma, and Birmingham, and the communities that impacted the civil rights legislation of the 1960s.[x] Not being afraid to fail is one of the things that is critical to leadership, and [to] making a difference in the world.

What does leadership mean to you?

It means representing for others what you want to see in the world. I think it means being willing to accept responsibility, even when responsibility can be overwhelming. It means reflecting the character and the values that you think are important for a healthy community. For me that includes compassion, and generosity, and kindness, and an open-mindedness to things that aren't always in harmony, but [that] need to be heard to be understood.

Leadership really is about making everyone understand common goals, common purpose, common objectives, and mobilizing people to achieve those things as much as you can.

What do you think the world needs more of?

I'm very concerned about this raging fear- and anger-politic. I think we need to all be resolved to pushing back against the politics of fear and anger. It will lead us into conflict, and controversy, and war, and crisis. There are so many things about which it's easy to be afraid. There are things that happen every day that will make you angry. We can't eliminate fear and anger from the human experience and the human psyche, but we can commit to govern ourselves as organized societies, as communities, as people, as families, in ways that are not shaped by fear and anger.

We need to be motivated by hope and by love. It sounds kind of simple, but it's actually pretty basic. If we're making policies because we're afraid, or because we're angry, if we're creating practices and laws rooted in fear and anger, we're at great risk of contributing to inequality and injustice. I think we're going to have to collectively, as a community, as a planet, begin to push back against that.

I was recently listening to someone whose perspective is much more cosmic. She talked about how, for her, it's helpful to sometimes take a different perspective. We're all on the planet Earth, so we're at least all earthlings as a starting point! And then we are other things. We are people who care about the survival of the planet; we can begin to create this whole new identity that I think can motivate us to achieve things that won't be achieved if we only think that we're in these small collections of entities that are at war or in conflict with these other entities. We have to really push back against fear and anger as a motivating and organizing force in the relationships between nations and communities.

What advice would you give your twenty-year-old self?

I would tell my twenty-year-old self to dream big. I didn't really imagine that I'd have the opportunities that I've had. It just, sort of, happened. It wasn't really something I thought about. I don't know that it would have made a difference had I thought more about it, to be honest. But I think it would have helped me to hear that I can achieve more than I've seen. It would've been helpful to have someone say, 'Oh no, you *should* have big dreams, and you *can* accomplish anything you want.' I would have told my twenty-year-old self, 'Don't be distracted by the things that are ugly and painful and hateful. You have to deal with them, you can't ignore them. But just stay focused on the things that are beautiful and inspiring and energizing, because ultimately those are the elements that will empower you to do the things that you need to do in the world. Dream big, dream big.'

'We have just allowed too many people in this country to be insulated from the pain, anguish and inequality that's created by mass incarceration. We have allowed too many people to be untouched by the burdens created by police. And when you break down those barriers, I think people are going to want to respond.'

About Bryan Stevenson

Bryan Stevenson is a public interest lawyer and founder of the Equal Justice Initiative whose work focuses on ending mass incarceration and excessive punishment in the USA. He was born on 14 November 1959 in a small, poor, rural town in Southern Delaware, USA. After being awarded a scholarship to Pennsylvania's Eastern University, he earned a Bachelor of Arts in philosophy in 1977. He later graduated from Harvard University in 1985 with a Master of Arts in public policy from the Kennedy School of Government and a Juris Doctor degree from the School of Law.

After graduating, Stevenson moved to Atlanta, Georgia, USA, where he worked as an attorney at the Southern Center for Human Rights. Here he began representing death row prisoners and capital defendants. In 1989 he founded a non-profit law centre called the Equal Justice Initiative (EJI) in Montgomery, Alabama, USA, where he acts as executive director. EJI aims to eliminate life-without-parole sentencing and capital punishment for minors and challenges racial discrimination in the criminal justice system. Stevenson and his staff have won relief, reversals or release for more than one hundred and thirty-five wrongly condemned death row prisoners.

In 2018, the EJI opened the Legacy Museum: From Enslavement to Mass Incarceration, in Montgomery, Alabama, both as a physical site, which is built on the site of a former slave warehouse, and as an outreach programme to educate and promote dialogue about America's history of racial injustice and its legacy of racial inequality; and The National Memorial for Peace and Justice, a six-acre memorial site constructed of over eight hundred weathered steel monuments – one for each county in the USA where a racial terror lynching took place, with the names of the lynching victims engraved on the column – where people can gather and reflect on America's history of racial inequality.

Stevenson is a Professor of Law at the New York University School of Law, and the author of *Just Mercy: A Story of Justice and Redemption* which has been on the *New York Times* bestsellers list for over one hundred and seventy consecutive weeks,[xi] and was released as a major motion picture starring Michael B. Jordan, Jamie Foxx and Brie Larson in 2020.

He has received numerous awards, including the a MacArthur Fellowship, the National Medal of Liberty from the American Civil Liberties Union, Public Interest Lawyer of the Year by the National Association of Public Interest Lawyers, the Olof Palme Prize for international human rights, the NAACP William Robert Ming Award for Advocacy, and the Benjamin Franklin Award for distinguished public service, as well as twenty-nine honorary doctoral degrees including degrees from Harvard, Yale, Princeton, and Oxford universities. He lives and works in Montgomery, Alabama.

eji.org

About the Project

'A true leader must work hard to ease tensions, especially when dealing with sensitive and complicated issues. Extremists normally thrive when there is tension, and pure emotion tends to supersede rational thinking.'

– Nelson Mandela

Inspired by Nelson Mandela, *I Know This to Be True* was conceived to record and share what really matters for the most inspiring leaders of our time.

I Know This to Be True is a Nelson Mandela Foundation project anchored by original interviews with twelve different and extraordinary leaders each year, for five years – six men and six women – who are helping and inspiring others through their ideas, values and work.

Royalties from sales of this book will support language translation and free access to films, books and educational programmes using material from the series, in all countries with developing economies, or economies in transition, as defined by United Nations annual classifications.

iknowthistobetrue.org

The People Behind the Project

'A good head and a good
heart are always a formidable
combination.'

– Nelson Mandela

A special thanks to Bryan Stevenson, and all the generous and inspiring individuals we call leaders who have magnanimously given their time to be part of this project.

For the Nelson Mandela Foundation:
Sello Hatang, Verne Harris, Noreen Wahome,
Razia Saleh and Sahm Venter

For Blackwell & Ruth:
Geoff Blackwell, Ruth Hobday, Cameron Gibb,
Nikki Addison, Olivia van Velthooven, Elizabeth Blackwell,
Kate Raven, Annie Cai and Tony Coombe

We hope that together we can help to mobilize Madiba's extraordinary legacy, to the benefit of communities around the world.

A note from the photographer

The photographic portraits in this book are the result of a team effort, led by Blackwell & Ruth's talented design director Cameron Gibb, who both mentored and saved this fledgling photographer. I have long harboured the desire, perhaps conceit, that I could personally create photographs for one of our projects, but through many trials, and more than a few errors, I learned that without Cameron's generous direction and sensitivity, I couldn't have come close to creating these portraits.

– Geoff Blackwell

About Nelson Mandela

Nelson Mandela was born in the Transkei, South Africa, on 18 July 1918. He joined the African National Congress in the early 1940s and was engaged in struggles against the ruling National Party's apartheid system for many years before being arrested in August 1962. Mandela was incarcerated for more than twenty-seven years, during which his reputation as a potent symbol of resistance for the anti-apartheid movement grew steadily. Released from prison in 1990, Mandela was jointly awarded the Nobel Peace Prize in 1993, and became South Africa's first democratically elected president in 1994. He died on 5 December 2013, at the age of ninety-five.

NELSON MANDELA
FOUNDATION
Living the legacy

About the Nelson Mandela Foundation

The Nelson Mandela Foundation is a non-profit organization founded by Nelson Mandela in 1999 as his post-presidential office. In 2007 he gave it a mandate to promote social justice through dialogue and memory work.

Its mission is to contribute to the making of a just society by mobilizing the legacy of Nelson Mandela, providing public access to information on his life and times and convening dialogue on critical social issues.

The Foundation strives to weave leadership development into all aspects of its work.

nelsonmandela.org

Notes

i   "Alabama ends death penalty by judicial override", *Associated Press*, 12 April 2017.

ii   State and local laws that enforced racial segregation in the southern United States from the 1870s until 1965.

iii   American spiritual song or hymn, "Wouldn't Take Nothin' For My Journey Now".

iv   Karl Paul Reinhold Niebuhr (1892–1971), American Protestant theologian and commentator. Niebuhr was quoting Pope John ("Let love be the motive and justice the instrument.") in an interview with American author and civil rights campaigner James Baldwin, about race relations in America in the aftermath of the 1963 bombing of the 16th Street Baptist Church in Birmingham, Alabama, USA, which killed four African American girls.

v   Martin Luther King, Jr. (1929–68), American Baptist minister and civil rights activist.

vi   The Equal Justice Initiative Legacy Museum, and the Equal Justice Initiative National Memorial for Peace and Justice in Montgomery, Alabama, USA.

vii   "My head is bloody, but unbowed", from the poem "Invictus" by British poet William Ernest Henley (1849–1903).

viii Václav Havel (1936–2011), Czech author, playwright and political dissident who played a major role in the Velvet Revolution that toppled communism in Czechoslovakia in 1989. Served as president of Czechoslovakia from 1989 until its dissolution in 1992, and president of the newly formed Czech Republic from 1993 to 2003.

ix   In his book, *Just Mercy: A Story of Justice and Redemption*.

x   The Albany Movement, Selma to Montgomery marches, and the Birmingham movement were nonviolent campaigns organized by Dr. Martin Luther King, Jr. and other civil rights groups to draw attention to racial segregation practices in the southern United States in the 1960s.

xi   At the time of printing, *Just Mercy: A Story of Justice and Redemption* by Bryan Stevenson has been on the *New York Times* bestsellers list in hardback and paperback for 172 consecutive weeks, https://www.nytimes.com/books/best-sellers.

Sources and Permissions

1   Jeffrey Toobin, "The Legacy of Lynching, On Death Row", *The New Yorker*, 15 August 2016.

2   Bryan Stevenson, *Just Mercy: A Story of Justice and Redemption*, (Scribe Publications, published by arrangement with Spiegel & Grau, an imprint of Random House, a division of Random House LLC, New York, USA, 2015), p. 314.

3   Ibid, p. 17.

The publisher is grateful for literary permissions to reproduce items subject to copyright which have been used with permission. Every effort has been made to trace the copyright holders and the publisher apologizes for any unintentional omission. We would be pleased to hear from any not acknowledged here and undertake to make all reasonable efforts to include the appropriate acknowledgement in any subsequent edition.

Page 6: "We need to talk about an injustice", Bryan Stevenson, TED2012, to watch the full talk visit TED.com; pages 13–14, 19: "The Legacy of Lynching, On Death Row", Jeffrey Toobin, *The New Yorker*, copyright © Conde Nast; pages 15, 17: *Just Mercy: A Story of Justice and Redemption*, Bryan Stevenson (Scribe Publications, published by arrangement with Spiegel & Grau, an imprint of Random House, a division of Random House LLC, New York, USA, 2015), copyright © 2014 Bryan Stevenson; page 38: "Civil rights hero Bryan Stevenson gets movie star moment with HBO documentary *True Justice*", John Anderson, *Los Angeles Times*, 26 June 2019; pages 51, 63: "Bryan Stevenson: the lawyer devoting his life to fighting injustice", Jamiles Lartey, *The Guardian*, 26 June 2019, theguardian.com/tv-and-radio/2019/jun/26/bryan-stevenson-lawyer-true-justice-just-mercy; pages 69–70: *Nelson Mandela by Himself: The Authorised Book of Quotations* edited by Sello Hatang and Sahm Venter (Pan Macmillan: Johannesburg, South Africa, 2017), copyright © 2011 Nelson R. Mandela and the Nelson Mandela Foundation, used by permission of the Nelson Mandela Foundation, Johannesburg, South Africa.

First published in the United States of America in 2020 by Chronicle Books LLC.

Produced and originated by
Blackwell and Ruth Limited
Suite 405, Ironbank, 150 Karangahape Road
Auckland 1010, New Zealand
www.blackwellandruth.com

Publisher: Geoff Blackwell
Editor in Chief & Project Editor: Ruth Hobday
Design Director: Cameron Gibb
Designer & Production Coordinator: Olivia van Velthooven
Publishing Manager: Nikki Addison
Digital Publishing Manager: Elizabeth Blackwell

Library of Congress Cataloging-in-Publication Data available.

ISBN 978-1-7972-0273-0

Chronicle Books LLC
680 Second Street
San Francisco, CA 94107
www.chroniclebooks.com

10 9 8 7 6 5 4 3 2 1

Manufactured in China by 1010 Printing Ltd.

Also available in the series: